MINNEAPOLIS & ST. PAUL
A PHOTOGRAPHIC PORTRAIT

PHOTOGRAPHY BY

James Kruger

NARRATIVE BY

Claire DeBerg

TWIN LIGHTS PUBLISHERS | ROCKPORT, MASSACHUSETTS

First published in the
United States of America by:

Twin Lights Publishers, Inc.
Rockport, Massachusetts 01966
Telephone: (978) 546-7398
www.twinlightspub.com

ISBN: 978-1-934907-42-9

10 9 8 7 6 5 4 3 2 1

(opposite)
Upper Saint Anthony Falls

(frontispiece)
Minneapolis Skyline

(jacket front)
Stone Arch Bridge

(jacket back)
Minneapolis Skyline and
St. Paul Winter Carnival

Image on page 68 used with
permission, Weisman Art Museum,
University of Minnesota.

Credit for artwork on page 39
Artist Oldenburg, Claes and
Coosje van Bruggen
Title *Spoonbridge and Cherry*
Date 1985-1988
Medium aluminum, stainless steel, paint
Dimensions 354 x 618 x 162"
Collection Walker Art Center, Minneapolis
Gift of Frederick R. Weisman in honor of his
parents, William and Mary Weisman, 1988
© Claes Oldenburg and Coosje van Bruggen

Book design by:
SYP Design & Production, Inc.
www.sypdesign.com

Printed in China

Combined, Minneapolis and Saint Paul make up the sobriquet Twin Cities, though you'll find they each have idiosyncrasies that establish them as distinct cities. The City of Lakes, Minneapolis, is the epicenter of the arts and the abode of sprawling parks encircling beloved lakes. Saint Paul, the capitol city, beckons visitors with majestic views of the Mississippi Riverfront and an epic historic district.

These side-by-side Minnesota cities are home to over 3.7 million people and boast one of the most culturally diverse metro areas in the US. This varied population means the culture of the Twin Cities is beautifully rich and lends them to an amazing art scene with world-renowned theatres, music, dance, fine art and literature along with extensive opportunities to enjoy miles of lakes and riverfront afforded by these rivertowns-turned-bustling-megalopolis.

Minneapolis & St. Paul: A Photographic Portrait is a beautiful visual reminder of the people who created the Twin Cities: the millers who channeled the waterfalls composing a global flour milling phenomenon out of Minneapolis; Theodore Wirth with his vision for a city with acres of protected park land; James J. Hill with his business acumen that extended the resources of the Twin Cities across the nation via railroads; Susan Ordway Irvine who inspired her Saint Paul community to support the creation of a vibrant performing arts center. These among so many others are the great minds that forged these cities.

Today, the people who honor that history with celebrations like the Winter Carnival and the Aquatennial allow visitors to appreciate what makes Minneapolis and Saint Paul such remarkable destinations. Indulge in this visual journey of James Kruger's elegant images of the Twin Cities, and then make your plans to visit them.

Gold Medal Park *(opposite)*

Designed by landscape architect Tom Oslund, this recent addition to the historic milling district has a 32-foot mound at its center, which was inspired by the burial mounds of Dakota Indians found throughout Minnesota. It overlooks the Mississippi River, the Stone Arch Bridge, and the Guthrie Theater.

AT&T Tower *(opposite)*

Featuring green and silver reflective glass, this 33-story building is located in downtown Minneapolis. Every water fixture in the building was retrofitted with efficiency models saving more than 13 million gallons of water each year. It houses AT&T, FICO and other offices, as well as a variety of shops and restaurants.

Hennepin Avenue Bridge

(top and bottom)

A modern suspension bridge, the Hennepin Avenue Bridge was completed in 1990 and is the fourth bridge at this location. The first bridge was completed in 1855 as a toll bridge and believed to be the first bridge to span the Mississippi River, thus garnering the title, "Gateway to the West."

Minneapolis Skyline

Skyscrapers emerged in Minnesota's largest city in 1886 with the construction of the first fireproof building in the US, the Edison Building. The city boasts 10 skyscrapers, three of which are among the tallest in the country. Most of the skyscrapers are linked by the world's largest pedestrian skyway system.

IDS Center *(top and bottom)*

Completed in 1972 at a height of 792 feet, architect Philip Johnson designed Minneapolis' tallest building with what he called "zogs," which allow for each floor to have 32 corner offices. The first seven floors, including a lobby and shopping area, are known as "Crystal Court."

Minneapolis City Hall *(opposite)*

Comprising an entire city block, the "Municipal Building" is an example of Richardsonian Romanesque architecture. Construction of this now historic landmark began in 1887 from granite blocks transported from Ortonville, Minnesota — some weighing as much as 23 tons. It is home to the world's largest four-faced chiming clock tower.

Boom Island and Lighthouse *(top)*

Situated above Nicollet Island and the St. Anthony Lock and Dam, this 14-acre riverside park was once a log sorting station for the logging industry. No longer a true island, the grounds are an attractive, accessible recreation area and a natural scenic overlook along the Heritage Trail.

Chain of Lakes *(bottom)*

One of the seven districts that make up the Grand Rounds Scenic Byway, this "City of Lakes" park system was formed in the early 20th century. It consists of 13 miles of public recreation trails around Lake Calhoun, Lake of the Isles, Lake Harriet, and Cedar Lake.

Mall of America *(above)*

Welcome to the largest shopping complex in the United States. Built in 1992, this expansive mall includes 520 retail stores, 50 restaurants, and the nation's largest indoor theme park. Without sales tax on clothing or shoes, the "MOA" is one of the world's most visited tourist shopping destinations.

Grand Rounds Scenic Byway *(opposite)*

A vision of Horace W. S. Cleveland in the late 1800s, today it is one of America's most important urban scenic byways. With 102 miles of trails comprised of 51 miles of walking trails and 51 miles of biking trails, the beautiful byway is made up of 4,662 acres of land.

Target Corporation (above)

Founded as Dayton Dry Goods Company in 1902 by George Draper Dayton, today Target is the second largest discount retailer in the U.S. and known for selling accessible goods at lower prices. Its headquarters, the glass building in the background, is on Nicollet Mall.

Foshay Tower (left)

Once the tallest building between Chicago and the West, the 1929 Art Deco Foshay Tower's design was inspired by the Washington Monument. Businessman Wilbur Foshay intended this to be his corporate headquarters and living residence, however, it was quickly lost to the stock market crash. Today, it is a W Hotel.

Wells Fargo Center (opposite)

Architect César Pelli designed this 1988 addition to the Minneapolis skyline. With a facade of buff-colored limestone and glass, this 57-story building has an indoor pedestrian promenade, a grand rotunda with a 100-foot-high ceiling, and has received numerous energy efficiency awards.

Mill City Museum *(above)*

Architect Tom Meyer incorporated the ruins of what was once the world's largest flour mill into this modern museum overlooking the Mississippi River. Through interactive exhibits, visitors learn about the milling industry that earned Minneapolis the nickname "Mill City."

Minneapolis Skyline *(opposite)*

Nearly every angle of the skyline provides a new perspective of Minneapolis — a city built around the power of water from St. Anthony Falls. Today, the city is headquarters to five Fortune 500 corporations: Target, US Bancorp, Xcel Energy, Ameriprise Financial, and Thrivent Financial.

Gateway Park and Fountain

This small downtown park and fountain were erected in proximity to the train depot so it would be one of the first things arriving train passengers would see upon entering the city. One of several fountains that beautify Minneapolis' parks, the Gateway Fountain illuminates with color each night.

Mary Tyler Moore Statue

Based on the opening scene from *The Mary Tyler Moore Show*, this beloved statue by sculptor Gwendolyn Gillen of Minnesotan Mary Tyler Moore tossing her hat into the air has been a Minneapolis icon since being installed in 2002. Visitors are encouraged to stop for a photo opportunity.

Lake Minnetonka *(above)*

Minnetonka is the Dakota word for "great water" which aptly describes this inland lake located 15 miles outside Minneapolis. With 125 miles of shoreline, it is one of Minnesota's most attractive lakes for fishing, boating, and recreation. A local legend reports a 10-foot sturgeon lurks beneath the surface of the lake.

Downtown Minneapolis *(left)*

Restaurants, retailers, theaters, and more are easy to get to, whatever the weather, with the city's eight miles of skyways. The first one opened in 1962, and today 80 blocks of buildings are interlinked by enclosed pedestrian footbridges.

Berger Fountain *(opposite)*

Benjamin Berger, a philanthropist and former park board commissioner, donated this playful fountain to the city. Known as the "Dandelion Fountain," it was installed in Loring Park in 1975 and was inspired by the El Alamein Memorial Fountain in Sydney, Australia's Fitzroy Gardens.

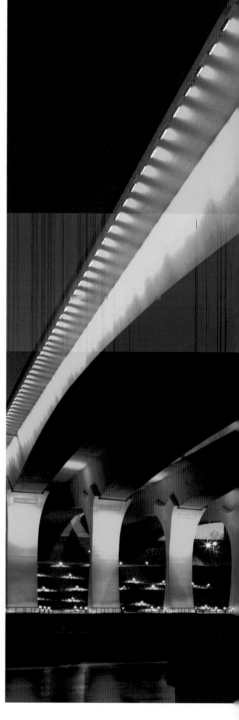

Calhoun Square *(top)*

This urban retail district is located at the intersection of Lake Street and Hennepin Avenue in the heart of Uptown, just minutes from downtown and adjacent to the Chain of Lakes. It's known for bustling vehicle and pedestrian traffic thanks to an eclectic mix of retail stores, entertainment, and restaurants.

CenterPoint Energy Torchlight Parade *(bottom)*

Since 1940 Minneapolis residents have been honoring its love of lakes with the Aquatennial, now a 4-day multi-event celebration. The festivities kick off with the largest nighttime parade in the state. Bands, floats, and entertainment march down Hennepin Ave. through the heart of downtown.

I-35W Saint Anthony Falls Bridge

Thirty bridges stretch across the Mississippi River throughout the Twin Cities. Most notably, the newly constructed I-35W bridge was erected in 2008 following a deadly collapse of its predecessor. Equipped with anti-icing sprayers and sensors that measure the condition of the bridge, it features decorative night lighting.

Mill Ruins Park

Flour produced in these mills powered by St. Anthony Falls in the 1800s was exported worldwide. Today's park is a result of an archeological study that unearthed the ruins of several abandoned mills. Located on the West Bank of the Mississippi River, it interprets the history of milling in Minneapolis.

Life Time Torchlight 5K *(top)*

One of many events during the Aquatennial — the annual civic celebration of Minneapolis — this summertime race begins at the historic Basilica of Saint Mary, passes through the heart of downtown Minneapolis, runs along the Mississippi River, crosses the Stone Arch Bridge, and ends in Father Hennepin Bluff Park.

Venice Mural *(bottom)*

Designed and painted by artist Hermann Krumpholz in 1992, this depiction of the famous Venice, Italy canals is on the brick wall of Gluek's Bar and Restaurant in the Warehouse District of Minneapolis. His oil paintings grace the walls of various restaurants, private homes, and public spaces throughout the Twin Cities.

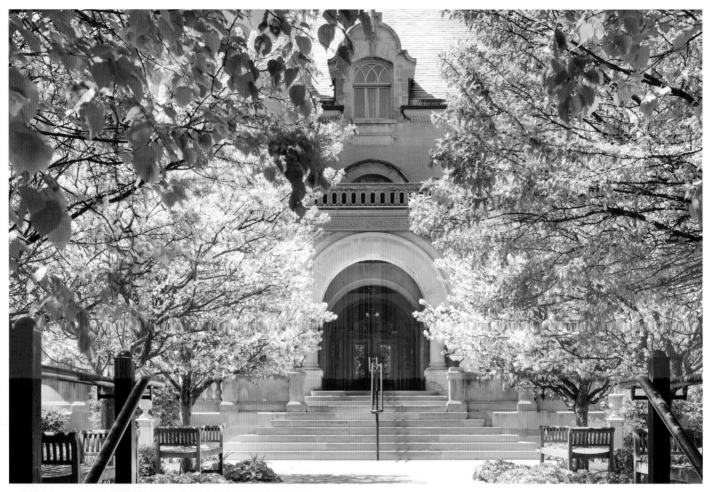

American Swedish Institute
Turnblad Mansion *(above)*

When affluent newspaperman Swan Turnblad donated his mansion on Park Avenue in 1929 it was the birth of what is now the American Swedish Institute. This historic museum celebrates Swedish heritage, migration, environment, contemporary Nordic culture, and art with engaging exhibitions and ongoing ties to Sweden.

Longfellow Statue *(left)*

Robert Jones commissioned this sandstone statue of Henry Wadsworth Longfellow in the early 1900s. While Longfellow, the American poet and linguist, never visited the area, learning about it inspired his poem *The Song of Hiawatha,* which brought Minneapolis' Minnehaha Falls global fame. Today, the statue stands in a restoration prairie.

American Swedish Institute Turnblad Mansion

This French Châteauesque mansion on 26th and Park Avenue in south Minneapolis took five years to complete. The detailed woodcarvings on the interior echo the equally exquisite stone carvings of the exterior. Swan and Christina Turnblad lived in the mansion from 1908 until 1929.

Bakken Museum *(top and bottom)*

Named after its founder, Minneapolis-native Earl Bakken, the co-founder of world-famous Medtronic, this museum is dedicated to STEM-focused educational programming, particularly the nature of electricity and Minnesota's med-tech industry. A Smithsonian affiliate, it is located in the West Winds mansion on Lake Calhoun.

Donaldson Mansion

Completed in 1906 for Lawrence Donaldson who, with his brother, founded Donaldson Department Store in Minneapolis, this historic home is the recipient of the Minnesota Preservation Award. It features ten fireplaces, stained glass, multiple terraces, and a carriage house connected to the main residence via tunnels.

Lakewood Memorial Chapel *(above)*

Inspired by Istanbul's Hagia Sophia, Minneapolis-based architect Harry Wild Jones designed this chapel, which became the nation's only pure example of Byzantine mosaic art. Completed in 1910, the 24 art nouveau stained-glass windows that circle the dome act as a sundial telling both the time of day and the season.

Lakewood Cemetery *(left)*

This serene, garden cemetery was established in 1871. It is comprised of 11 miles of manicured roads, an eight-acre lake, and 250 acres of grounds. Some of the many famous people laid to rest here include Hubert H. Humphrey, Paul Wellstone, Curt Carlson, T. B. Walker, and Tiny Tim.

Garden Mausoleum and Reception Center

This contemporary design includes an outdoor contemplation garden, winding paths, benches, and the Pool of Reflections. The building itself fills with natural light and was constructed with granite, wood, and marble with onyx accents combined to create an inviting space of reflection and care.

Fort Snelling National Cemetery

Originally established in 1870 at a nearby location as a burial ground for 680 soldiers who perished at Fort Snelling, their remains were moved to this location in 1939 when the Fort Snelling National Cemetery was officially established. Today, these 436 acres are the resting place for 208,000 individuals.

Minnehaha Depot *(top)*

Opened in 1875 and servicing passengers until 1920, this depot was designed in the Carpenter Gothic style of architecture featuring gingerbread ornamentation and other delicate detailing along the roofline. Just 22x20 feet, this is the first railroad line west of the Mississippi River that connected Minneapolis with Chicago.

Minnesota Streetcar Museum
(bottom)

An experience not to miss, the restored and operating fleet of six historic Minnesota streetcars offer visitors a unique look at streetcar use and history. The Como-Harriet Streetcar Line runs between Lake Harriet and Lake Calhoun for a refreshing view of life in the early 20th century.

Minnehaha Falls

Near the confluence of Minnehaha Creek and the Mississippi River these falls attract nearly 900,000 visitors annually. Translated from Dakota words for water *mni* and waterfall *ȟaȟa*, the Minnehaha Falls have a 53-foot drop and can be viewed from the bridge above it or from trails that lead to the gorge on both sides.

Hiawatha and Minnehaha Statue

Jacob Fjelde's most famous statue was inspired by Henry Wadsworth Longfellow's poem, *The Song of Hiawatha*. Created in plaster in 1893, the fictional woman, Minnehaha, is depicted being carried by her lover, Hiawatha. The statue was recast in bronze in 1912 and is placed on an island near Minnehaha Falls.

The Time Being (opposite)

Paul Granlund, a native Minnesota artist, has over 650 sculptures around the world as he was a prolific, sought-after sculptor. Bronze figures being his signature modus operandi, Granlund created *The Time Being* in 1973 for the Federal Reserve Bank in downtown Minneapolis. It features a nude man stepping from a bronze mold.

Metro Minneapolis (above)

The metro area of Minneapolis is home to 3.7 million people and is considered a global city because of its contribution to the world's economy through the many Fortune 500 companies headquartered here. Its cultural organizations support diverse theatre, visual art, dance, writing, and music exhibitions and performances.

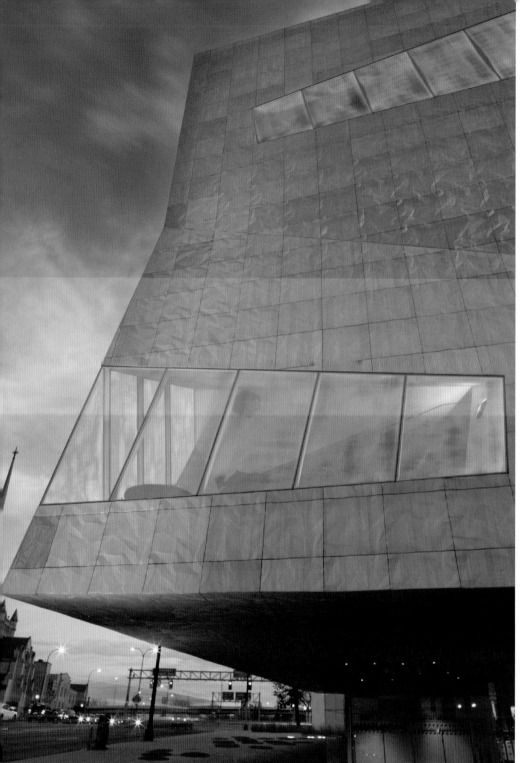

Walker Art Center

Opened in 1927, this public gallery is one of the five foremost modern art museums in the country. It offers visual and performing art experiences, film and video, educational programs, and free admission every first Saturday. Over 700,000 people visit the Walker annually.

Spoonbridge and Cherry

Artists Claes Oldenburg and Coosje van Bruggen created this playful iconic symbol as the centerpiece to the Minneapolis Sculpture Garden. Installed in 1988, this beloved sculpture was crafted from aluminum and stainless steel, and features water flowing over the cherry and mist rising from its stem.

Guthrie Theater (above)

Along the exterior of the Guthrie Theater are several large panels that display photographs of some of the world's greatest playwrights and founder Sir Tyrone Guthrie. They include August Wilson, Lorraine Hansberry, Tennessee Williams, Arthur Miller, Anton Chekhov, Eugene O'Neill, and George Shaw.

Guthrie Theater (left)

The brainchild of Sir Tyrone Guthrie, this center for training, education, production, and performance is a world-renowned resident theater. Designed by Jean Nouvel and completed in 2006 at a cost of $125 million, it houses three theaters and the 178-foot "Endless Bridge" which extends to the Mississippi River.

The Times They Are A-Changin' *(above)*

This famous son of Minnesota graces the wall of an art deco building in downtown Minneapolis on Hennepin and 5th street. Brilliant Brazilian artist Eduardo Kobra and crew transformed a whitewashed wall with portraits of Bob Dylan at various stages In hls career. *The Times They Are A-Changin'*, was completed in 2015.

Mayo Clinic Square *(right)*

Formerly known as "Block E," this site sits across the street from Target Center—home to the Minnesota Lynx and Timberwolves. Outside, the redesigned space is aesthetically aligned with the city's modern approach to architecture, while inside the clinic brings Minneapolis world-class, comprehensive sports medicine care.

Minneapolis Central Library *(top)*

With over 2.4 million items including books, DVDs and music, the Minneapolis Central Library offers the third largest per capita library collection in the United States. Designed by César Pelli and opened to the public in 2006, it features an 18,560 square-foot "green" roof planted with sun- and drought-resistant ground cover.

Minneapolis Convention Center *(bottom)*

The Upper Midwest's largest convention center, the MCC has 475,000 square feet of exhibit space. This environmentally sustainable space boasts a rooftop solar array of 2,613 panels, which produces 750,000 kWh of renewable electricity per year, the equivalent of powering 85 homes.

Orchestra Hall *(opposite)*

Since it opened in 1974 as the home for the Minnesota Orchestra, this cultural hub and architectural wonder has hosted more than 10 million people at its concerts. Renovated in 2013, the more than 100 large cubes in the auditorium enhance the acoustics throughout the concert hall.

Children's Theatre Company *(top)*

This regional state theatre draws families from across the state for engaging performances often cast with young adult performers. It was established in 1965 and has been called "The #1 children's theatre in the nation," by *Time* magazine. Its productions, workshops, and camps aim to challenge, educate, and inspire the community.

MacPhail Center for Music *(bottom)*

Established in 1907 by William S. MacPhail, today it enrolls over 14,500 students, ages 6 weeks to over 100 years old, in musical education. The modern building was designed by James Dayton and the center was one of the first schools in the nation to introduce the Suzuki method of music.

Gold Medal Park *(opposite)*

Situated in the Mill District neighborhood, this green space in downtown Minneapolis was specially designed with an inviting spiral walkway, luminescent benches, and 300 trees. It is a lovely 7.5-acre urban park with the nearby Remembrance Garden — a tribute to the 13 victims of the 2007 I-35W bridge collapse.

Lake Calhoun

Originally known by the Dakota as *Mde Maka Ska*, which means "White Earth Lake," this lake is entirely surrounded by city parkland and a popular spot for kayaking, canoeing, and windsurfing. With a 3.4-mile trail for biking, a 3.2-mile trail for walkers and runners and three swimming beaches, it has something for every visitor.

Midtown Greenway

Used by 5,000 people on busy days, the Midtown Greenway is a 5.5-mile system of bicycle and walking trails in south Minneapolis. Constructed on a former railroad corridor, today it connects with all the major trail systems in the city. They are lit at night, plowed in winter, and open all day, everyday.

Lake Calhoun

With the backdrop of the Minneapolis skyline, Lake Calhoun is a gorgeous urban water body. It hosts a yacht club, sailing school, athletic fields, parking, picnicking areas, boat races, road races, boat docks, archery spaces, boat launch, boat rentals, and Tin Fish — a restaurant featuring seafood and fish tacos.

Lake Calhoun *(top)*

Canoeing and kayaking in Minneapolis are a must. Lake Calhoun and Lake of the Isles were connected by a canal so adventurers can start at the Calhoun boat docks, paddle the canal, explore Lake of the Isles' islands, enjoy the serenity of Cedar Lake, and finally rest at Brownie Lake Park.

Nice Ride Bike Rental *(bottom)*

Nice Ride Minnesota is a non-profit providing public bike sharing in the Twin Cities and greater Minnesota. Any member can take a bike from its 190 bike stations and return it to any of the stations. More than 1.8 million riders annually take advantage of this urban bikeshare system.

Lake of the Isles Winter Fun *(top)*

Skating on a Minnesota lake, a quintessential winter experience, is possible since Minneapolis has three lakes that offer lake skating. There are 47 rinks at 22 different parks throughout the city, including Lake of the Isles.

Lake of the Isles *(left)*

Minneapolis parks receive 21.4 million visits each year. One reason to visit its lakes is to find where "Minne the Lake Creature" is spending her summer. She bears a striking resemblance to the Loch Ness Monster and when spotted she brings smiles to visitors young and old.

**Upper St. Anthony Falls Lock
and Dam** *(above and right)*

This lock and dam on the Mississippi
River was completed in 1963 and
accounts for over 10% of the total
river height changes between the
Twin Cities and St. Louis. The Lower
Lock and Dam, along with this one,
span the river's only waterfall along
the Mississippi's length of 2,320 miles.

Stone Arch Bridge

James J. Hill built this former railroad bridge, and at its peak it ushered 80 passenger trains daily into Union Station. It ceased operation in 1965 and in 1989 Hennepin County purchased it for $1,001. Lit from beneath, it is the only arched bridge made of stone anywhere on the Mississippi River.

Stone Arch Bridge (top)

Built with Minnesota native granite and limestone, this majestic 1883 bridge is one-of-a-kind offering panoramic views of St. Anthony Falls and the Minneapolis skyline. Measuring 2,100 x 28 feet, there are 23 stone arches linking the Father Hennepin Bluff Park with the Mill Ruins Park on the West Bank.

Fireworks (bottom)

Every July Minneapolis residents join the official civic celebration — the Aquatennial — an annual series of festivities. The 4-day event, "The Best Days of Summer," culminates with the Target Fireworks display — one of the top five firework shows in the United States and with the best viewing from the Stone Arch Bridge.

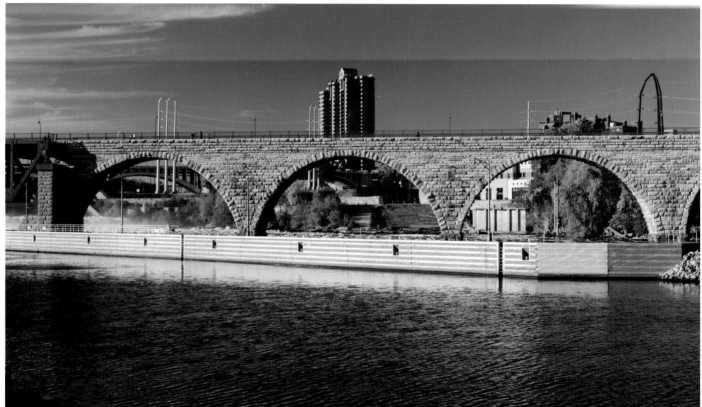

Stone Arch Bridge (top)

In 1980 the rehabilitation of this registered National Historic Engineering Landmark began. While no longer a railroad bed, today's traffic across the bridge is mostly walkers, runners, and cyclists. The bridge is open year round with guided tours of the bridge and St. Anthony Falls.

St. Anthony Falls and Stone Arch Bridge (bottom and opposite)

This pedestrian and bicycle bridge is now part of a two-mile walking tour. The St. Anthony Falls Heritage Trail is an extensive system of interpretive signs sharing historic stories and pictures. It encompasses Nicollet Island, the Hennepin Ave. Bridge, West River Parkway, historic Main St., and the Mill District.

Cedar Lake (opposite)

Named for the red cedar trees that once grew along its shores, there are three popular beaches found here and one, nicknamed "Hidden Beach," is only accessible via a forest trail. The Cedar Lake Regional Trail is 3.5 miles of bicycle and pedestrian paths connecting St. Louis Park with Minneapolis.

Lake Minnetonka (above)

In 1880, one of the nation's largest hotels at the time, Hotel St. Louis, opened on Lake Minnetonka with 200 rooms and accommodations for 400 guests. While today there are no hotels on the lake, the area is populated with luxury homes.

Lake Minnetonka (pages 58–59)

This is Minnesota's ninth largest lake and was officially named in 1852 using the Dakota's descriptive phrase *Minn-ni-tonka*, meaning "big water." The 1906 "streetcar boat" *Minnehaha* was raised from the bottom of the lake in 1980 and after restoration it has resumed carrying passengers between Excelsior and Wayzata.

Lyndale Park Gardens *(top and bottom)*

Tulips and flowering trees make this park a springtime destination. Adjacent to Lake Harriet, Lyndale Park's 61 acres are enjoyed year round as walking paths take visitors through the second oldest public rose garden in the United States.

Lake Harriet Band Shell

(top and bottom)

Minneapolis residents have the gift of free outdoor music thanks to "Music in the Parks," a 1892 initiative which continues today. The Lake Harriet Band Shell is the signature venue for this annual live music series featuring jazz, swing, folk, rock, classical, and more at public parks around the city.

Theodore Wirth Statue Garden *(left)*

Theodore Wirth was instrumental in designing the extensive Minneapolis park system. In 2004, this sculpture by Bill Rains was erected near the Theodore Wirth Parkway, which shows Wirth surrounded by 12 children. It honors his policies, which pushed for equal access for all people regardless of race or economic status.

Theodore Wirth Golf Club *(right)*

One of the oldest public golf courses in the state, it offers rolling hills, lagoons, beautiful skyline views, mature trees, and Bassett Creek on the front nine. Completed in 1916, the park board voted to allow free play during the first year. In its inaugural year 12,000 rounds were played.

Lyndale Park Gardens *(opposite)*

Under the direction of park superintendent Theodore Wirth, the garden's first rose garden was planted in 1907 by horticulturist Louis Boeglin. Today, the park features the Annual-Perennial Garden, the Butterfly and Hummingbird Garden, the Perennial and Border Garden, the Peace Garden, and the Rose Garden.

Phelps Fountain (top)

The Phelps Fountain, known as "Turtle Fountain," was installed in 1963 in the Lyndale Park Annual-Perennial Garden. A gift from park commissioner Edmund Phelps, carved in the column is an Indigenous person, a cleric, a lumberman, a factory worker, and a woman with two children. The base features turtles spouting water.

Nicollet Island (bottom)

The Sioux used this island as a birthing place, a vision quest destination, and a neutral meeting place. Named after French explorer and cartographer Joseph Nicollet who mapped the Upper Mississippi in the 1830s, it is comprised of a high school, an inn, three multi-family units, and 22 restored Victorian-era houses.

Segway Tours (above)

A fun way to tour the historic sites, amazing architecture, beautiful river-fronts, and green spaces of both Minneapolis and Saint Paul is gliding atop a Segway. This clean air alternative to tour buses gets visitors up close to all the sights the cities have to offer.

Nicollet Mall (right)

The first transit mall in the nation, Nicollet Mall is distinguished by the 12 blocks of stores that run down the center of Minneapolis. Closed to automobile traffic, it features a pedestrian-friendly design. There is also a free Metro Transit bus that runs up and down Nicollet Mall everyday.

Minneapolis Institute of Art (above)

Officially opened in 1915, "Mia" welcomes more than 700,000 visitors each year. It is a pillar of culture with a permanent collection of over 83,000 objects spanning 5,000 years including photographs, textiles, architecture, contemporary art, Asian art, drawings, paintings, and more.

Museum of Russian Art (right)

Open to the public in 2002, the museum has extensive collections of Russian and Soviet art including paintings, Russian orthodox icons, Soviet stamps, textiles, lacquer art, photography, and Matryoshka dolls. It hosts lectures, seminars, and events featuring Russian cultural experts.

St. Mark's Episcopal Cathedral (opposite)

This 1910 architectural gem on Hennepin Avenue overlooks Loring Park. With majestic stained-glass windows and detailed carvings throughout the sanctuary, St. Mark's offers a respite from the bustle of the city. The church is committed to work and pray for peace, justice, and reconciliation.

DERICK R. WEISMAN ART MUSEUM

Weisman Art Museum (pages 68–69)

Designed by architect Frank Gehry, this teaching museum is a landmark on the campus of the University of Minnesota. Its stainless steel skin — an abstraction of a waterfall and a fish — reflects the light around it. The museum houses 20,000 works of art from American Modernism to Korean furniture and beyond.

The Science Teaching and Student Services Building (top)

Its design inspired by the Mississippi River, this University of Minnesota building was awarded LEED gold certification for its environmentally designed construction. Most source materials were obtained from manufacturers within a 500-mile radius of the campus to support the regional economy.

University of Minnesota (bottom)

The University of Minnesota was founded in 1851 and today is a public research institution of higher education. There are five campuses, nearly 70,000 students, and 25,000 employees. Notable alumni include eight Nobel Prize laureates, two United States vice presidents, and two Pulitzer Prize winners.

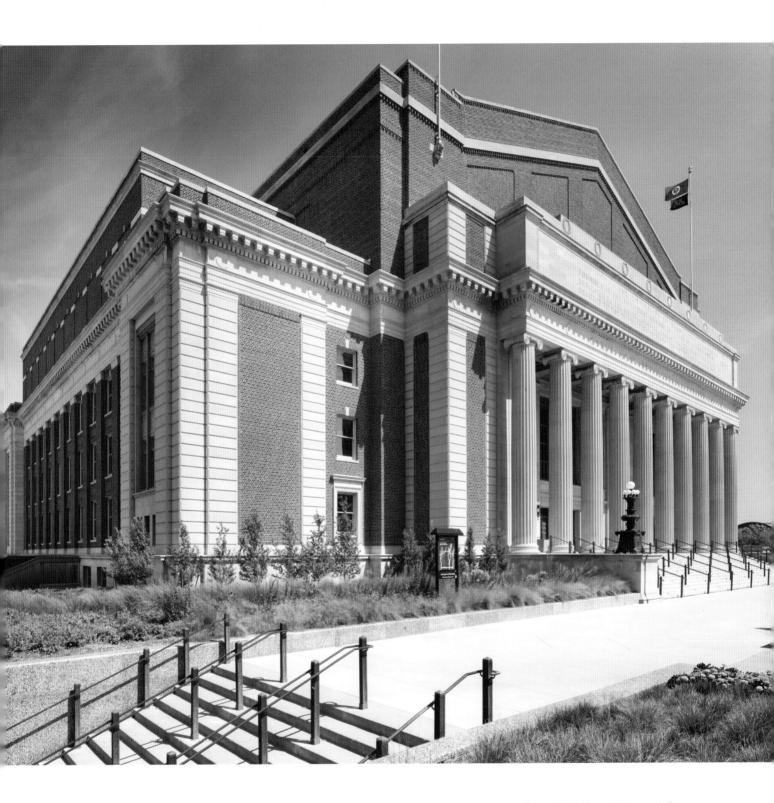

Cyrus Northrop Memorial Auditorium

This Classical Revival performing arts venue on the University of Minnesota campus is host to rock concerts, ballet performances, and grand lectures. Built in 1929, it seats 2,700 people and houses one of the largest pipe organs built by Aeolian-Skinner still in existence.

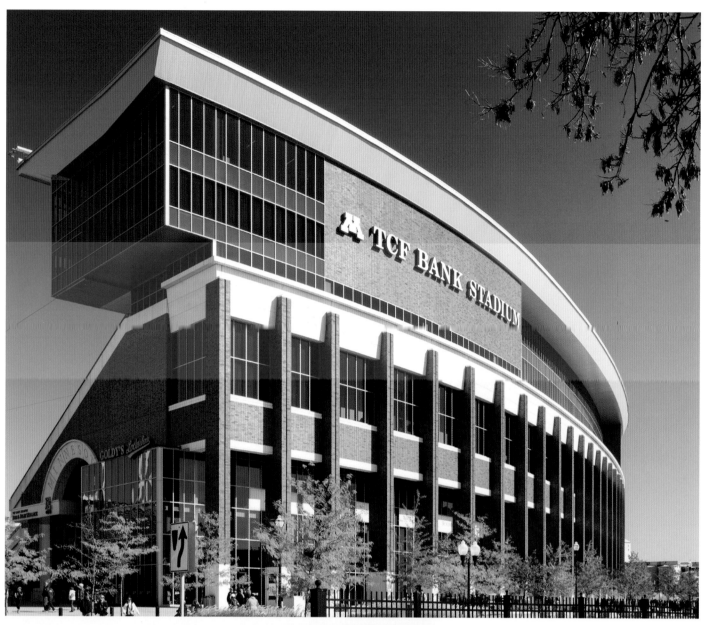

TCF Bank Stadium *(above and left)*

Home to the Minnesota Gophers football team, this 52,525-seat stadium at the University of Minnesota Minneapolis campus, opened in 2009. To acknowledge the stadium as a facility for statewide use, the names of Minnesota's 87 counties are individually carved in stone on the perimeter of the first level.

U.S. Bank Stadium

Built on the previous site of the Hubert H. Humphrey Metrodome, this 73,000-seat stadium is the new home to the NFL's Minnesota Vikings. It features a translucent roof and movable front windows, allowing fans to view downtown Minneapolis as well as receive protection from rain and snow.

Target Field *(above)*

Located in the Warehouse District of Minneapolis, this is the home ballpark of the Minnesota Twins baseball team. Built with local Kasota limestone, the stadium seats over 39,000 fans and offers heated viewing areas as well as a heated field.

Rod Carew *(left)*

Hall of Famer Rod Carew played for the Twins between 1967 and 1978 before being traded to the Angels. This bronze statue, which portrays his unique batting stance, is one among several statues depicting famous Twins and officials. Other Hall of Famer Twins include Bert Blyleven, Kirby Puckett, and Dave Winfield.

Target Field (above)

This new outdoor park was welcomed by fans as they had previously shared space in the Hubert H. Humphrey Metrodome with several other sports teams. In 2010, the first baseball park made expressly for the Minnesota Twins opened and has been called the #1 baseball stadium experience on the continent.

Harmon Killebrew (right)

Sculptor Bill Mack created this bronze of the great Harmon Killebrew as well as the other Twins figures located outside of Target Filed. Killebrew played for the Twins from 1961–1974 and was inducted into the Hall of Fame in 1984.

Target Field

Nestled in the heart of downtown Minneapolis, this 8.5-acre field is enclosed on four sides by a highway bridge, two rail lines, and an interstate making it easily accessible to fans. At night, color-changing lights reflect off a wind veil facing the field offering a subtle calm to the field.

Minnesota Zoo (top)

The Minnesota Zoo in Apple Valley, Minnesota opened in 1978 and was one of the first zoos to organize its animals by the environments in which they lived, rather than by species. The six-themed exhibit area is home to 4,700 animals, many of which are endangered.

Minnesota Zoo (bottom left and right)

Over the years, the zoo has been acknowledged as a world leader in conservation. Today, visitors can get a close look at a Siberian tiger or ring-tailed lemur, both on the endangered species list, as well as see other exotic and rare animals.

Minnesota Zoo Discovery Bay

Home to sharks, fish, and coral, a spectacular floor-to-ceiling viewing area welcomes visitors to observe the Shark Reef and the zoo's most colorful creatures on the Discovery Bay — one of six trails at the zoo. Every year 1.2 million guests enjoy this zoo — the state's largest environmental educator.

Mississippi River *(pages 80–81)*

The Mississippi River and Saint Paul are seen here blanketed in a soft, pink glow at sunrise. An abundant source for many, nearly 260 different fish species can be found in the river and 60% of all North American birds use the river as their flight path.

Saint Paul City Hall and Ramsey County Courthouse *(above)*

Built during the Great Depression in downtown Saint Paul, this magnificent Art Deco building houses county, city, and state offices. Bas-reliefs adorn the limestone exterior and the interior features a Memorial Hall with white marble floors, three stories of black marble piers, and a gold leaf ceiling.

Saint Paul Riverfront

Nestled along the Mississippi River, the Twin Cities are located just nine miles from each other with wonderful parks, lakes, and recreational opportunities. With a combined population of 3.7 million, Minneapolis and Saint Paul form a beloved megalopolis.

Skygate (opposite)

Designed by R. M. Fischer and unveiled in 2000, this stainless steel and acrylic sculpture towers in downtown Saint Paul. Inspired by the legendary winter ice palace and garden gateway structures, Fischer created it for the "New Millennium" project. At night the acrylic sphere glows blue and, combined with the rings, represents infinity.

Sky (above)

Georgette Sosin created *Sky* from welded aluminum. Placed on the Kellogg Mall Park in 1981, it is one of several of her works located around the state. Sosin is originally from Strasbourg, France. She and her husband open their Minneapolis studio to the public during events like "Art-A-Whirl."

Mitchell Hamline School of Law
(above)

Formed in 2015 by the merging of William Mitchell College of Law and Hamline University School of Law, it offers more enrollment options for students than any other law school in the US. It started as a night school in 1900 by five Saint Paul lawyers.

Landmark Center *(opposite)*

This historic 1902 building originally served the entire state of Minnesota as the city's post office, courthouse, and custom house. Today, this Romanesque gem is a center for cultural art and also houses a cafe, gift shop, gallery spaces, and a visitor center.

Minnesota History Center

(above and opposite)

Both a library and a museum, the Minnesota History Center opened in 1992 and houses a vast collection of historic books, letters, records, art, photographs, and more. The center is also the state's premier presenter of historical exhibits, with more than 800,000 people visiting it annually.

Ordway Center for the Performing Arts

The brainchild of 3M heiress Sally Ordway Irvine, this world-class, not-for-profit performing arts venue opened in 1985. With over 500 performances each year, the opportunity to experience professional dance performances, concerts, educational programs, and more is always available.

Raspberry Island Regional Park

Situated in the Mississippi, this is the last true island in Saint Paul. Visit it via the Riverwalk parkway to see the beautiful landscape of Saint Paul's downtown. With a quaint band shell, it hosts "Music in the Park" in the summer and is a popular location for weddings and celebrations.

Minnesota Children's Museum *(above)*

In operation since 1981, this downtown museum engages young minds with exciting, interactive exhibits that encourage play and discovery. Children are inspired to touch, climb, and splash their way around this well-designed and imaginative museum.

Peanuts Sculpture *(left)*

In 2000, "Peanuts on Parade" was launched to honor Charles Schulz, the hometown cartoonist of *Peanuts*. The tribute began with 101 five-foot-tall Snoopy statues across the city. For four subsequent years a different character was on display. Proceeds from auctioned statues helped create permanent bronze statues, including Peppermint Patty's best friend, Marcie.

Minnesota Transportation Museum
(above)

Opened in 1999, this fascinating museum is dedicated to preserving the machines and history of local buses, trains, and streetcars. Each Saturday the museum offers train rides from the historic 1907 Jackson Street Roundhouse — one of the last of its kind in the nation and built by "Empire Builder" James J. Hill.

Railroad Charlie *(right)*

On loan to the Transportation Museum, Susan Otterness's "Railroad Charlie" greets visitors with open arms, a striped engineer's hat, and a bright yellow scarf. This statue is just one of the many fiberglass *Peanuts* statues throughout Saint Paul.

Science Museum of Minnesota

Founded in 1907, today's museum features exhibits covering natural history, technology, physical science, and mathematics. *Iggy*, a 40-foot iguana made of railroad spike heads, greets visitors before they enter the museum. Sculptor, Nicholas Swearer was only 15 when he completed it in 1971.

Science Museum of Minnesota

Among the many resident exhibits at this museum is "Dinosaurs & Fossils" featuring a Triceratops and the "Native American Exhibition" with artifacts from the Dakota and Ojibwe people. It also features the first ever theatre in the northern hemisphere with a rotatable dome: the IMAX Convertible Dome Omnitheater.

Minnesota State Fair

(pages 96–97, above, and left)

Known as "The Great Minnesota Get-Together," this state fair is the largest in the US given its average daily attendance, the highest being over 250,000. This 12-day fair features livestock and cooking competitions, various foods on a stick, entertainment, and the "Princess Kay of the Milky Way" butter sculpture.

Mickey's Dining Car (above)

Since opening in 1937, this historic diner has been operating nonstop in this 50x10 foot-long, Art Deco-style dining car. From its downtown location, diners enjoy old fashioned malts and shakes—hand-dipped and blended on a spindle along with "Mickey's Sputnick" double-decker burger or the "Classic" cheeseburger.

Japanese Lantern Lighting Festival
(pages 100–101)

Frog Pond is aglow with Japanese lanterns at Como Park. Modeled after the Japanese Obon festival that honors ancestral sprits, this summer festival includes drumming, origami demonstrations, music, dancing, and more. It culminates at dusk with the lighting and release of paper lanterns.

Charlotte Partridge Ordway Japanese Garden

(above, left, and opposite)

The people of Saint Paul's sister city, Nagasaki, Japan, gifted this garden's design to the city. It is meant as a peaceful space for respite and retreat. Masami Matsuda, the architect of the landscape, created it in a "strolling pond" style featuring rocks, plants, water, paths, and lanterns—all elements of peace.

Majorie McNeely Conservatory

(above and left)

Featuring two acres of gardens under glass, this jewel of Saint Paul opened in 1915. One of the most beloved buildings in the city, it is a warm getaway in the winter and an inviting lush, setting in the summer.

Como Park Zoo & Conservatory
(right)

A free zoo and conservatory that began in 1897 with just three deer, Como Park welcomes more than 1.9 million visitors each year to enjoy the large cat exhibit, aquatic life displays, primates, birds, a world class polar bear exhibit, as well as brightly colored flamingos.

Book Bench *(opposite top and bottom)*

Created by Geri Connelly, this playful sculpture can be enjoyed at Phalen Poetry Park — a free community garden and park. The grounds are designed to appear like a giant sleepy dragon. Benches in the shape of open books dot the walking paths. One path leads to the *Poetry Post* listing local poets.

Man-Nam *(above)*

Located at the Governor's Residence, is Paul Granlund's Vietnam memorial, *Man-Nam*. Erected in 1970, this full-length nude man with outstretched arms appears to have emerged from a sheet of bronze. Granlund was known for his striking sculptures that combined human and geometric forms.

F. Scott Fitzgerald House *(opposite)*

Known as "Summit Terrace," this historic home at 599 Summit Avenue is part of a row house built in 1889. Recognized for being the residence where Fitzgerald completed his first novel, *This Side of Paradise*, Fitzgerald periodically injected his hometown of Saint Paul into his fiction.

F. Scott Fitzgerald Statue *(left)*

Part of the "Lost Generation," Fitzgerald is best known for his novel *The Great Gatsby*. Even in his short life (he died at age 44) Fitzgerald published numerous short stories and four novels as well as writing in Hollywood for Metro-Goldwyn-Mayer. This bronze statue by Michael Price stands in Rice Park.

Anthrosphere *(right)*

On display at Wells Fargo Place, Minnesota artist Paul Granlund's sculpture invokes movement and life. Creating a sphere, figures representing the world's seven continents are connected by ocean masses. Sea life is embedded on the masses and the bodies appear in the same formation as the continents on the earth.

James J. Hill House (top)

Built in 1891 for railroad magnate James J. Hill, this house is a US National Historic Landmark. The Rich-ardsonian Romanesque architecture lends itself to the exceptional location, which towers over Saint Paul and the Mississippi River. It includes intricate detailed woodwork from the formal dining room to the music room.

Minnesota Governor's Residence (bottom)

This historic English Tudor was built in 1912 for the Horace Hills Irvine family. It sits on 1.5 acres and features 20 rooms: nine bedrooms, eight bath-rooms and nine fireplaces. Located at 1006 Summit Avenue, "The Gov-ernor's Mansion" is the home of the Governor and family.

Summit Avenue Historic Hill District (opposite)

Part of two national historic districts, the homes along Summit Avenue in Saint Paul are distinct for their grandi-osity having been built between 1890 and 1920 in the Late Victorian style of architecture. A fashionable place to live, the neighborhood boasts landmark homes, cathedrals, and synagogues.

Cathedral of Saint Paul (left and right)

Situated high atop Cathedral Hill, this historic cathedral has a commanding view of Saint Paul. It is one of the largest cathedrals of Beaux-Arts architecture in the US. Completed 1915, it features a large blue, stained-glass window over its front doors and a warm, decorative interior.

Church of St. Agnes (opposite top)

Created to welcome the German-speaking Austro-Hungarian population of immigrants in the early 1900s, this classic Baroque style church features a beautifully detailed dome. Rising 60 feet above the floor, its mural portrays Christ crowning Agnes of Rome. The vault is covered in decorative scroll work.

Church of Assumption
(opposite bottom)

This 1865 church retains much of its original decor and is the oldest church still standing in the state of Minnesota. Located in downtown Saint Paul, it has four bells that can be heard from every corner of the city.

Korean War Memorial *(opposite)*

This eight-foot statue of an infantry soldier approaching an archway by sculptor Arthur H. Norby symbolizes the 94,646 Minnesotans who served in the Korean War. It is located on the mall of the capitol and honors "all who gave some — some who gave all."

Fort Snelling *(top)*

Overlooking both the Mississippi and Minnesota rivers, this fort was constructed in the 1820s, decommissioned in 1946, and today serves to educate visitors about those who lived in and near the fort. Costumed staff share the fort's history, including an Independence Day Celebration featuring the boom of cannon salutes.

Minnesota State Capitol *(bottom)*

Memorial Day flags dress the grounds of the Minnesota State Capitol Mall. Self-guided tours of the grounds include war memorials for the veterans of WWII, Korea and Vietnam; a commemorative garden honoring Minnesota suffragists; and several sculptures of famous Minnesotans like Charles Lindbergh and Leif Erickson.

Minnesota State Capitol

Towering above the southern entrance of the Capitol is a gilded quadriga, *The Progress of the State*, sculpted by Daniel Chester French and Edward Clark Potter. Four horses represent the powers of nature: earth, water, fire, and wind. Two women leading the horses symbolize civilization, while the man riding in the chariot represents prosperity.

Minnesota State Capitol

This unsupported marble dome is crafted after Saint Peter's Basilica in Rome. It is the second largest in the world and from the grounds has an expansive view of downtown Saint Paul. Much of the interior is crafted from pipestone, which was used by the Indigenous people of Minnesota for creating peace pipes.

Padleford Riverboats *(above)*

Board historic riverboats from Harriet Island in Saint Paul and traverse the mighty Mississippi River. Riverboats journey along scenic routes to places like Pig's Eye Cave, the Saint Paul High Bridge, Fort Snelling, and Pike Island — all along the 72-mile river park: The Mississippi National River & Recreation Area.

Lock and Dam No. 1 *(opposite)*

There are 29 locks and dams for barge tows along the Mississippi River, beginning in the Twin Cities and ending in the Gulf of Mexico. Each year 2 million tons of cargo passes through this lock, just one of the steps in the "stairway of water" that makes barge travel possible.

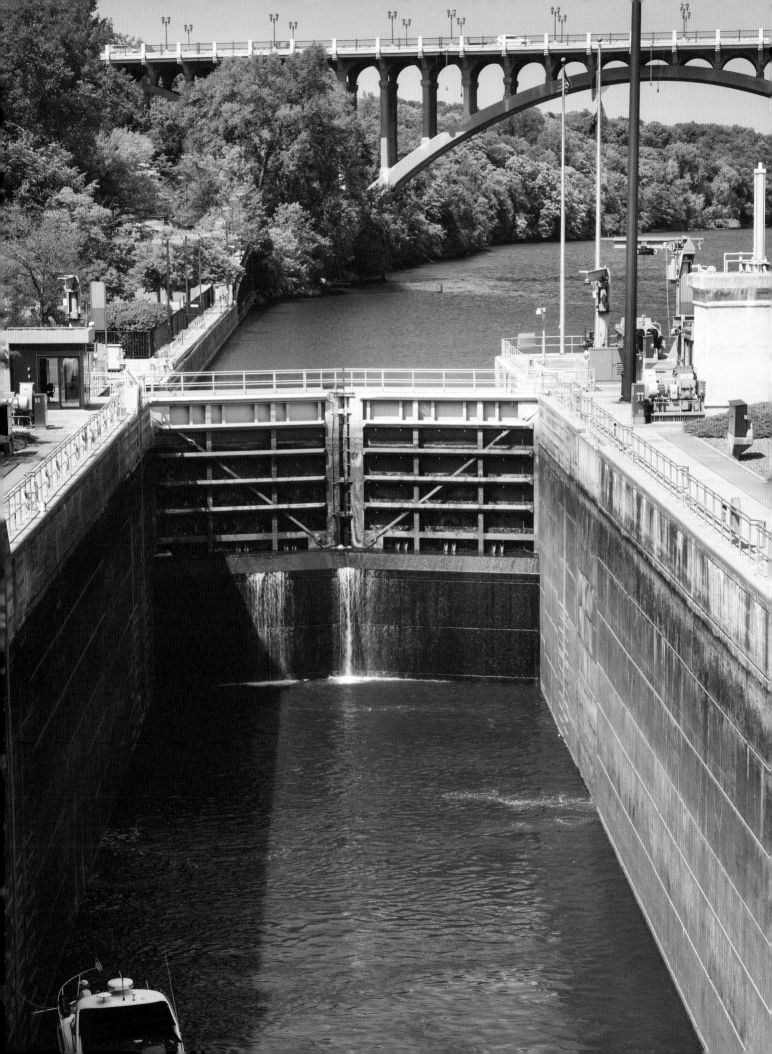

St. Croix River *(top and bottom)*

The majority of this 164-mile long river creates the border between Wisconsin and Minnesota. It joins the Mississippi River near Prescott, Wisconsin. French for Holy Cross, the St. Croix River is a National Scenic Riverway. One hydroelectric plant on the river supplies power to the Twin Cities.

St. Croix River

Once a major route for logging, the St. Croix welcomes recreational use from fishing and boating to camping and canoeing. Just 30 minutes from downtown Saint Paul, it is host to nearly a dozen state parks and is protected by the National Wild and Scenic Rivers Act of 1968.

Alexander Ramsey House *(opposite)*

Built in 1868 for the second governor of Minnesota, Alexander Ramsey, it is one of the most pristinely preserved Victorian homes in the country. There are year-round tours, the most popular of which is during Christmas where the table is set with the family's china, and a tree is decorated with the family's ornaments.

St. Croix River *(top and bottom)*

With over one hundred miles of river to enjoy, the chance to encounter wildlife is great. Bald eagles fish along the banks as do herons and dozens of other bird species. Other wildlife like mink, fox, whitetail deer, black bear, and beaver rely on the St. Croix for food.

St. Croix River (top and bottom)

Several Indigenous tribes, namely the Ojibwe and Dakota, once occupied the surrounding St. Croix River Valley. Today, several bridges span the river including state highways and the Stillwater Bridge, a vertical-lift bridge between Stillwater, Minnesota and Houlton, Wisconsin where an average of 18,000 vehicles cross every day.

Wabasha Street Caves (opposite)

Built into mines carved from sandstone, Wabasha Street Caves date back to the 1940s. Today, it is an event hall and tourist destination in downtown Saint Paul, but was once upon a time home to gangsters, speakeasies, a river refuse collection site, and even a mushroom garden.

Saint Paul Winter Carnival

(above, right, and opposite)

The "coolest celebration on Earth" since 1886, this two week carnival celebrates the beauty of Minnesota winters with an ice palace, a citywide treasure hunt, giant snow slides, parades, autonomous snowplow competitions, snow sculpting, music, food, ice carvings, and more.

James Kruger. Jim Kruger is a Twin Cities-based commercial photographer specializing in architecture, people, travel, nature, and stock photography. With more than 20 years of experience as a working creative photographer, Jim's portfolio for regional, national, and international clients includes advertising, corporate, portrait, editorial, and hospitality assignments.

He has a passion for exploring and photographing the outdoors, whether he is shooting a landscape on the cliffs of the Nā Pali Coast or right in his own backyard along Minnesota's North Shore. Jim is an owner/partner of LandMark Photography — a studio specializing in architectural interiors and exteriors, commercial real estate, and aerial photography — and a licensed commercial pilot. Learn more about Jim's work at kruger-images.com or landmark photo

Claire DeBerg. Raised in the enchanting hamlet of Ham Lake, Minnesota, Claire is honored to claim as home what she aptly refers to as the "Midcoast." A ballerina with a fondness for typewriting, she graduated from the Perpich Center for Arts Education in dance then went on to get her BA in English from Bethel University. After receiving her master's in Creative Writing, she was a Professor of English, and then in 2007 launched a successful writing agency in Minneapolis. The spunk and wit of her two children, Gloria and Harold, and her husband Darren's venturous approach to life, illuminate Claire's writing personality. To learn more about Claire's writing and modeling, visit clairedeberg.com